PRAISE FOR D.

"Kristin is a fearless and badass entrepreneur. Her no-BS take on how to run a successful business has made me a stronger, more courageous leader who's ready for anything."

SAMANTHA (SAM) ANDERSON
CO-FOUNDER & COO, 41 ORANGE

"As a woman, it is often difficult to have a voice that gets heard and respected, both professionally and personally. Dr. K provided me with the megaphone needed to amplify my voice, daily inspiration to propel my success, and the unconditional support of a true mentor and coach. When all else fails, she stands beside me with her middle finger in the air to all those who try and bring us down! No one is better at so eloquently and perfectly telling others to fuck off than Dr. K!"

ANGIE SURRA
VP COMPLIANCE & TECHNOLOGY, NAVIGATEHCR

"Dr. K is a complete rockstar, a wildly successful business owner, coach, and mentor. My business grew by 30 percent in revenue after my time working with her through a coaching and mentoring program. She's got creative solutions and really thinks outside of the box in everything she does, from business to building her tribe and community, to giving back to others as a top-line priority, to wild adventures with friends. Dr. K takes life to the next level and is a true inspiration."

LEAH NOLAN
CEO, STORM BRAIN

"Dr. K is the businesswoman young female entrepreneurs need in their corner. She is a champion at encouraging women to run their lives, businesses and teams and stand strong in their power."

KELLY DUFORD
DUFORD LAW

"Dr. K has been instrumental in the growth and success of my business. Not only is she a strategic leader who has built and sold a number of businesses, but she also makes it a point to give back to other business owners and women leaders. She has incredible drive and is always willing to help and include others."

ANNA CROWE
FOUNDER AND CEO, CROWE PR

MOTIVATION

M̶O̶TIVATION

USE THE POWER OF "NO" TO MAKE YOUR FIRST MILLION DOLLARS

DR. KRISTIN KAHLE

MERACK PUBLISHING

NOTIVATION

USE THE POWER OF NO TO MAKE YOUR FIRST MILLION DOLLARS

Published and distributed by Merack Publishing

Cover and interior design | Yvonne Parks

Library of Congress Control Number: 2020910225

Kahle, Kristin,

ISBN 978-1-949635-44-7 (eBook)
ISBN 978-1-949635-43-0 (Perfect bound)

DEDICATION

To all of the people who told me NO in my life.
I couldn't have done it without you fuckers.

Thank you.

TABLE OF CONTENTS

INTRODUCTION

WTF IS NOTIVATION?

Hi. I'm Dr. Kristin Kahle (say it like the salad or the smoothie if that's your thing). Or call me Dr. K.

I have a story for you.

Once upon a time, my brother was dying, and I had the power to save his life. But the world tried to tell me NO; the world said I wouldn't be allowed to save him. I saved his life anyway. Jason is still alive today and lives every day like it might be his last.

A few years later, when I was in elementary school, educators branded me a "special learner" and told me I'd never amount to anything. Consistently, over and over, the world said NO to my academic dreams. I earned a doctorate anyway.

When I was 19, I fell in love with an older man. He assaulted me and beat me up. It was my first lesson that sometimes the world violently says NO to love. I put him in jail. And then I forgave him. Today I'm happily married.

After college, I went into business with my dad. It was great for a while. And then my dad said NO (a long story that I'll tell you in the next chapter) to my growth. So I started my own company—in a highly male-dominated industry—and made my first million dollars at age 28.

Then I sold that company and started another one. I took it to a million dollars within a year. And then I did it again.

WTF is NOtivation? For me, NO is motivation. Being told NO by the world is the very thing that motivated (or NOtivated, if you will) me to become part of the less than five percent of women business owners who earn $1M+ in annual revenue.

Do you want to know how I did it? Want to learn how to do it yourself? I want that for you, too, because I think women like us are sick of being told NO by the business world. Let's change it.

Read on, sister.

THE FORMULA

ME+NOTIVATION=YES

The title of this chapter cracks me up, because, really, math (especially algebra) and I are not friends, although I have developed my version of an equation for success.

My formula is pretty simple. Tell me no, and I'll do it anyway. And I'll do it in a bigger and more badass fashion than if I hadn't been told no in the first place.

My formula is made up of what I like to call Dr. K's Nine NOtivational Nuggets. These are my core values, my principles, my own ground rules that I never waiver from and are at the heart of my success. And they are, I think, valuable to every woman doing business in a world where the rules (and the power to say no) are primarily still in the hands of men.

Now, don't get me wrong. I like men. I've worked with them and for them, I've mentored them, and I'm happily married to one. I'm also a female entrepreneur who's kicked ass in a traditionally male industry, and I'm here to tell you, women are still being told NO in ways that simply don't happen to men.

That's where the Nine NOtivational Nuggets come in. I'm going to get to them shortly, but first, I want to share some of my story, which will give you context and understanding about why the Nuggets work for me and can work for you as well.

DOING BUSINESS IN A MAN'S WORLD

When I say I've spent my career in a male-dominated industry, I mean it. Let me bore you with my bio for a second, just for fun.

> In 1990, Dr. Kristin Kahle (me) began her
> insurance career on the Sales Management
> Team at John Hancock Insurance Company
> in Boston, MA. Since then, she has served in
> a variety of capacities for companies including
> Leavitt Group (National Restaurant Division,
> Vice President), PIS (Vice President), Intercare
> Insurance Services (Vice President), SFG
> Benefits Insurance Services (Vice President of
> Marketing and Operations), and Lincoln Life

Insurance Company (Employee Benefits and Client Services Manager).

Dr. Kahle received her Doctorate in Business Administration (DBA) from Argosy University, where she was the first Doctoral candidate to write a dissertation on Healthcare Reform (ACA). Dr. Kahle also holds a Master of Business Administration (MBA) from University of Phoenix and a Bachelor of Arts (BA) in Business Administration from Pine Manor College in Chestnut Hill, MA, where she was the only female basketball player to score over 1,000 points and get over 1,000 rebounds. Today, Dr. Kahle is a Certified Healthcare Reform Specialist (CHRS), a nationally recognized speaker and educator on all areas of compliance, and has been awarded "Most Influential Woman in Benefits" in both 2014 and 2015 by Employee Benefit Advisor.

With more than 20 years of industry experience, Dr. Kahle founded NavigateHCR (NHCR), a full-service Affordable Care Act (ACA) and compliance consulting company that offers a variety of services to assist employers and brokers with even the most complex requirements of laws governing employee benefits. NHCR was founded in 2012 and is the oldest ACA technology and compliance company in the country. With a sole focus on simplifying compliance, NHCR acts as an extension to HR Departments in order to lessen the burden on employers of time-consuming processes, distribution of required employee communications, and complicated reporting.

Sexy, huh? The truth is I've wanted to work in the bright lights and magic (kidding) of the insurance world since I was a kid. In fourth grade, I wrote a paper about how I wanted to be in the insurance business with my dad. That fourth-grade paper is framed and hanging on my office wall today.

All I knew then was that my dad's job got us cool trips to Europe and other exotic places.

What I know now, of course, is that insurance and especially compliance (stop yawning, I have a point) are critically important to employers who want to stay in business. I founded NavigateHCR to protect American employers and American jobs and make compliance fun and easy. We've done that.

And now, as I'm transitioning from running NavigateHCR to educating and mentoring others, I'm often asked to tell my own story about how I made it to where I am and how I did what I did.

And that—the thought of getting up on a stage (or any forum) and sharing my personal story—can be terrifying!

After all, the traditional business world separates the personal from the professional. Everybody knows that feelings (not my favorite "F" word, by the way) have no legitimate home in the workplace, right? I mean, we've all heard the saying, "It's not personal, it's just business."

At work, logical thought supersedes feelings. Nearly every woman in business has experienced or watched someone else get hit with negative consequences for emotional displays in the workplace.

Really, to me, workplace disregard for the emotion and feelings that shape all of us are just one of the gender stereotypes that keep many women in business playing small and taking NO for an answer.

But guess what? We humans can't set an intention without emotion. As I said, I started my last company to protect American businesses and their employees. There was emotion—giving, the desire to help people—in that intention. Have I made a shit-ton of money doing it? Yes. And I have also improved the lives and business practices of a shit-ton of people.

So anyway, I digress. After spending decades in an industry where I'm STILL often the only woman in the room and seeing the value in moving beyond that workplace division of personal and professional, I'm now sharing my story.

Why? Because it turns out we humans are inspired and motivated—wait, maybe NOtivated—by the transformational stories of others.

So I decided to be transparent and vulnerable and tell it all—the anger, the hurt, the fuck-ups—all of it.

A TINY PINK STIFF-ARM

I'm the youngest child in my family and the only girl. My brother Tim is four years older than me, and Jason is three years older, so when I came along, my mom was really ready for a girl. She recently told me she spent forty bucks (a lot of money in the 70s) on a pink dress to take me home from the hospital in.

Mom took me home in my girly outfit, sat down to cuddle with me, and, as the story goes, my little baby arm came out and pushed her away. Apparently, my independent streak was fully-formed at birth, and I'm still that way. I mean, I'll hug it out, but I'm not much into cuddling.

Today, I'm six foot two, my favorite "F" word is fuck, and I've spent my life playing with the boys.

Hell, I started early by saving the life of one of them.

LIKE TWINS

In 1978, my brother Jason woke up with a mysterious black eye. He was seven years old. The eye wouldn't heal, and Jason was soon diagnosed with aplastic anemia, a condition that can occur when the body stops producing enough new blood cells. It is rare, and back then was almost always fatal. The doctors told my parents that Jason had six months to live.

We lived in Toledo, Ohio, which offered no medical alternatives for Jason. However, a new treatment for Jason's condition, a bone marrow transplant, was being performed at the University of Minnesota Medical Center.

At the time, only 25 bone marrow transplants had been completed in the United States. Jason would be number 26, and just 12 of the patients had survived, so this was serious, scary stuff.

Here's a funny story, though, just to break up this dark mess. My family is Catholic, and when my mom and Jason moved to Minnesota to do the transplant, my mom approached a nun and said, "I really want to give Jason daily communion. We don't know if he's going to live or die. He needs to have communion every day."

The nun and the priest said, "You are not a participant in our church, and therefore we're not going to give your child communion every day."

So, my mom did the logical thing. She broke into the church and stole a bag of host (for non-Catholics, 'host' is what we call communion wafers). True story. My mom stole from a church.

Anyway, the medical professionals told my parents the only way that Jason would survive was if someone in the family perfectly matched his human leukocyte antigens.

My oldest brother Tim was nine at the time, and he wanted so much to be Jason's match; they were fourteen months apart, he loved his brother, they were best friends. He prayed and pleaded to be his match. But Tim wasn't a match.

They tested my parents. Parents are not necessarily matches either.

So they tried me. At the time, I was a little feisty four-year-old curly-haired girl. I was a perfect match—so much so that Jason and I could have been twins.

Great news, right? Except Jason had to wait for a bed in Minnesota (meaning, sadly, that someone else in the transplant system had to die).

In the meantime, the state of Ohio objected to my parents "using" me as a donor to save my brother's life, and I became a ward of the state. That was a big, fat NO to both me and Jason.

I was shipped off to live with my grandparents, my mom and Jason went to Minnesota, and my dad and older brother stayed in Toledo. We became a family divided.

I didn't realize what was happening, of course. I was four. All I knew was that my parents and brothers—the people I loved—were totally gone from my life.

If that wasn't enough, the state put me in therapy. I met weekly with the psychologist assigned to me (in my memory it seems like daily), who asked me at every single session, "Do you want to save your brother's life?" I think, as ridiculous as it sounds now, that they wanted to be sure my parents weren't coercing me and that I was making up my own mind (again, I was FOUR).

I remember being pissed off about it. I distinctly remember the psychologist making it seem like my parents were pushing me to be a bone marrow donor for my brother. And the truth is, there was never any discussion from my parents, from my brothers, from my grandparents, from my aunts.

Nobody really talked about it around me. I'd walk into a room, and there'd be hushed conversations, right? Or the grownups would tell me to go outside and play. I don't think I understood the magnitude of it all. I just understood that I loved my brother, he was going to die, and I held the keys to his life.

I'd had the pre-tests, the docs had told me that I could save Jason's life, they'd explained all of the potential traumas that could happen while I was in surgery, and had warned me about the pain.

I thought all the talk and time wasted was stupid. I think for me, even at just four years old, my frustration was really more about, "Why are we even having this discussion?"

Evidently, at some point, the state of Ohio was convinced, and we began the transplant process. Jason was admitted to the hospital and received total body radiation. In radiation lingo, 1,000 rads is fatal. Jason received 759. Imagine making that decision as a parent.

NEEDLES AND HAMMERS

Jason was readied, and I flew to Minnesota from Ohio for my part of the bone marrow transplant. I was on one floor of the hospital, and Jason was on another. I had my transplant team, Jason had his team, and we had one primary doctor—Dr. John Kersey, MD—who oversaw both of us.

They say a bone marrow transplant is really easy to do. Maybe it's easier now, but I'm here to tell you that back then it was a five-hour brutal procedure. I was awake, laying on my stomach, and they hammered a huge needle—over and over—into the bones in my back.

My marrow was sucked into three IV bags for transplant to Jason.

It was barbaric. I had this bonnet thing around my little head, and I was face down, so I couldn't really see anything. My parents could see into the room, but I couldn't see them, and they couldn't come in.

My mom told me that when I was finished with the procedure, Dr. Kersey gave each of them an IV bag, and the three of them—mom, dad, and the doc—prayed over the bags as they rode the elevator to Jason's floor.

I was released the day after in a wheelchair and sent back to my grandparents in Ohio.

What I didn't know is that when I got back to Ohio, I would have to start a process of injections to speed up my bone marrow regeneration in case Jason rejected the first batch.

So, every two days, I went to the doctor for shots. I continued to live with my grandparents because my mom was in Minnesota with Jason; his survival required that he lived inside a bubble for an extended time at the hospital. My dad and Tim were in Toledo, so I had little to no relationship with my immediate family. In 1978 there were no cell phones, no Internet. We couldn't FaceTime or video chat.

Finally, Jason was released from the hospital after spending one entire year there—from the time he was eight until he was nine. We were all in Minnesota for his release and together as a family for the first time since his diagnosis.

Jason finally got to go outside! Our family was all kinds of awkward because we'd been apart so long, but we decided to celebrate by going to the park for a picnic.

I was five at the time. Jason was bald, very sickly, and there was a little boy at the park giving my brother a hard time, making fun of him, telling him he can't go down the slide.

So I picked up a giant stick and hit that kid. Of course I did. After all that? You don't tell me, or my brother, NO.

The transplant was a monumental thing—for science, for me, and of course for Jason. Jason is still alive and doing amazing things with his life!

BACK TO NORMAL

When we got back home, however, people KEPT telling me NO.

We were the local Toledo freak show for a long time. We had the cancer kid. Nobody wanted to see the cancer kid. The local newspaper had written a lot of articles about us. We retreated for a while and isolated ourselves to protect our family. We just wanted to be normal.

That didn't happen.

After Jason's release, we moved to a new house. A new address meant new schools, and new schools hurled me into all kinds of fun adventures with the word NO.

YOU WILL NEVER...

Remember when I said earlier that math and I are not friends? Yeah. Well, that message showed up in second grade in the form of a teacher named Mrs. Pruder. What a bitch. (Sorry/not sorry if that offends you. But she was.)

Second grade is probably the worst year I've ever had in my life because I could not grasp multiplication. About a week into the school year, Mrs. Pruder told me, "You are NEVER going to amount to anything if you're not able to do multiplication."

She said it every day, or at least that's how it seemed to me. By the way, when Mrs. Pruder retired shortly after second grade, the school gave her a money tree. I told the principal they should take that money back because she didn't deserve it. She was a terrible teacher.

I had a learning disability—dyslexia with letters and numbers—and this was long before the Individualized Learning Programs of today. In the 70s (and I KNOW this is not PC or even kind, but it's the truth) they sent me to what everybody called the 'Tard Bus.

The "Learning Van" was for special learners. I went there for reading and I went there for math. Every day I'd have to put my coat on, walk out to the learning van past the windows with everybody looking at me, and then walk back in. Being the feisty girl I was, I hated it, and I didn't want to do it.

I went back into the Catholic school system in fifth grade. Basically, every single teacher at my other school had told my parents that I was never going to read or do math properly, so they decided to send me to a school called Mary Immaculate. It was well known as a Special Ed school for special children.

I went to Mary Immaculate for fifth grade, and after a year, the teachers said, "She shouldn't be here. We're going to skip her a couple of grades." (Eye roll.) Obviously, I didn't fit there, either.

For seventh and eighth grades, I went back into the mainstream Catholic school system. I struggled with math. I struggled with reading. And I think I probably struggled with time management.

At Saint Joan of Arc, I began to explore athletics, and I had tutors and teachers who would let me do extra credit. Can you imagine that I needed extra credit to get a grade of D or D-minus? I did. That extra credit kept me from flunking.

But I was starting to have fun, and things were looking up. We were beginning to see possibilities in the way I learned. Maybe, just maybe, there were some YES answers on the way.

OR NOT...

In eighth grade, I was required to take a placement test to get into the Catholic high school.

I flunked the test. Not only did I fail it, I completely fucked it up.

The principal at Toledo Central Catholic called my dad and told him they weren't going to let me in. My dad and I went in to talk to him. The principal and my dad knew one another, and my dad didn't think they would reject me because we were a legacy family and my parents could afford the tuition.

But NO.

The principal said, "We can't let her in. She basically only scored her name right on the test. That's all we can give her points for."

Well, I got upset, which is so funny to me now because I never get upset. But I knew I was not going to argue about it. I pointed my finger at the principal and said, "I'm going to this high school, and then I'm going to college, and you are letting me in!"

They allowed me to retake the test, which didn't go any better. I think I actually lost points. My parents took me around to other high schools in the area, and we talked about tutors.

But I knew, I always knew that I would go to the same high school that everybody in my family—and I mean everybody: my brothers, dad, uncles, cousins, grandparents—attended. It never dawned on me that I would go anywhere but Toledo Central Catholic. There was no question for me.

To this day, I'm not sure how it happened (probably because we were legacy), but eventually I got into Toledo Central Catholic high school.

AND THEN...

High school offered three learning tracks: AP, College, and Gen Ed. Well, as you know, I WAS going to college, so I chose the college track, which required algebra, geometry and a foreign language.

My learning disability, which was still unrecognized at the time, took me right back to the learning van. What do you think I did? I skipped going to the learning van. I wasn't walking past the windows in sight of everyone.

I was labeled "Non-College Bound" as a freshman because I couldn't pass algebra and repeatedly told—again—that I would never get into college.

I was passing some of my classes, like social sciences and geology, because they tested differently.

My parents sent me to multiple classes to learn how to study, how to read, how to extract stuff from a sentence, how to test. But I couldn't comprehend algebra and geometry. My brain just wouldn't get there.

I couldn't do a timed test; when you have dyslexia, and you don't understand a question, you have to re-read it over and over. Of course, I always ran out of time.

But I did learn time management in high school. I didn't have a choice, really. I would get up an hour before school, go to study table (some schools called it study hall), work my way through ten different classes (three of which I was flunking), and depending on the season, I played volleyball, basketball or track. On game days, I also had to go to mass. At night I'd go home and work with a tutor. And then do it all over again the next day.

With all of that, I should have been acing my classes, but because of the way I learn, none of it was getting through.

And even with all of this fucking effort, my counselors were still telling me NO, you'll never get into college without algebra.

Well, who needs algebra anyway? Nobody uses it. I've never used it. With tutors and summer school, I finished high school with a 1.3 GPA.

Even so, I DID go to college. And I killed it.

COLLEGE MADE SENSE

After tons of research on schools that specialized in learning disabilities, I enrolled at Pine Manor College in Brookline, Massachusetts.

I excelled there. I became an avid reader. I found business courses. They made sense to me.

But algebra still didn't, and I had to pass it freshman year. I went to the algebra teacher, Dr. Stein, and said, "Okay, here's what's up. I will show up. I will always show up. I will always come to class. I will not skip. I will never grasp what the hell you're talking about, but I will always be here. So what's my percentage for participation, and what's my percentage for attendance?" I'd figured out that if I showed up, I could at least start with a C or C minus.

She said, "Okay, I know you're working through this. I will give you the test as many times as you need to take it throughout the entire semester."

I eventually passed the test, whether through my effort or Dr. Stein's grace, I'll never know. My freshman year GPA was 2.0 tops.

But by senior year it was a totally different story! I graduated college with a 3.97 and was inducted into Alpha Chi sorority. What happened? Why the radical change?

I took business courses that I loved. I fell in love with statistics and became a statistics tutor. I even earned an accounting award.

I also picked up field hockey and lacrosse (because the skirts were cute). Oh, and not inconsequently, I'm still the only student in the school's basketball history to have over 1,000 points and 1,000 rebounds.

DREAMS COME TRUE

Not long after I graduated from college, my brother Jason got a residency in San Diego. My mom and I went out to help him get settled and pick out couches and towels and all the things that boys don't do when they move into a place, right?

It was January, sunny and 72 degrees, and we loved it. My mom picked up the phone, called my dad and said, "Sell the house. Sell the business. We're not coming home."

True story. The whole family moved. My dad commuted between San Diego and Ohio and eventually sold the house and his business so we could be there permanently.

I was studying for my MBA while working various jobs—at a bank, in retail, as a lifeguard. After I completed my MBA, I went to work for a company called California Fringe Benefits (CFB), which was a Lincoln Life Company. It was my second insurance job; I had worked at John Hancock during my undergrad at Pine Manor.

When my dad decided to start a new employee benefits business in San Diego, I applied to work with my dad. That's right. I APPLIED to work for my dad's company.

I was actually up against other candidates; my dad didn't give me the job instantaneously because I was his daughter. He made me earn it, including calling my references and negotiating my salary.

I told him I would do anything but sales. I didn't want to sell because I was young and didn't know how to live on a commission-only salary. So for about eight months, I did account management, service, training. I basically ran the account management side. My fourth-grade dream come true!

I had such a great time, and eight months in I decided to jump into sales. I saw an opportunity for a mid-market person. Turns out I'm good at sales.

And then that NO thing showed up again.

ARE YOU FREAKING KIDDING ME?

About two years into all of this fun and success, my older brother Tim moved to California. He and my dad decided Tim would be joining us in the business.

Decided, right? Tim didn't apply. Tim wasn't required to interview, supply references, or negotiate his salary. My dad brought him in as a partner at the same ownership level as me. He was not licensed and, unlike me, gave my dad a list of all the things he WOULDN'T do in the business.

Talk about being told NO! It fucking pissed me off beyond belief, because I had EARNED my success for two years. Tim had some life issues, including alcoholism. He was drinking on the job. In true passive-aggressive sister fashion, I used to dig his alcohol bottles out of the trash and his desk drawers and put them on my dad's desk.

I don't know if it was his intention or not, but Tim got back at me. He was handling much of the back end stuff, including payroll. While I was on a 17-day open-enrollment tour (for my dad's largest client), which included something like 14 flights and 22 meetings, my brother decided to withhold my paycheck.

One night I found myself in the middle of one the Dakotas, standing at a hotel front desk and unable to check in because I had no money in my account. My card was declined, and by the way, I was fronting the money for this trip.

I called my dad, because you know that's what a girl does. She calls her dad to try and bail her out. My dad—also my boss—took care of it and said, "I don't understand why you have no money." I didn't either. I should have been paid.

I got home five days later after enrolling 22,000 employees, and Tim's excuse was that he didn't pay me because I hadn't submitted an expense report. WTF? So ridiculous.

My dad was fine with Tim's decision. I told him he should have had my back and he didn't. And not just because I was his daughter. He should have had my back as an employee who was out doing company business. It wasn't like I was partying on vacation.

I felt like my dad chose Tim over me, and as hard as it is to say, I think it was partly because I'm a girl and the baby of the family. That's when I knew my dad was telling me NO, too. And that was when I knew it was time to leave the family business.

NOTIVATION

My dad's decision NOtivated me right into starting my own firm, Glass House Benefits and Administrators. My last name was Glass at the time (I had a young, dumb, and relatively short first marriage), and I started the business out of my house. Hence Glass House. (See what I did there?)

My dad and I devised a plan so I could take some clients and buy some clients. Yes, correct. I bought some clients, and I also sold my ownership back to my family. I was barely scraping by, doing odd jobs here and there, cocktail waitressing and doing anything I could to get by in San Diego, which is challenging to do.

I ultimately grew the business doing fun and exciting insurance things, and eventually, another company came along and wanted to buy me out.

I was in a place of "great, this is where I want to be" and went to work for another company that ended up buying my dad's company, as well. So there we were, all working together again: me, my dad, and Tim.

I left that company six years later, started my second company doing consulting, and decided to get my Ph.D. I guess I was still proving wrong every single teacher and administrator who told me I would never amount to anything.

I married my second husband, Hector, in 2011, and we're still going strong today!

DR. K MEETS THE ACA

While I was consulting and working on my doctorate, the Affordable Care Act (ACA) passed. Being the overachieving insurance nerd that I am (and now an avid reader…take that teachers!) I decided to read the ACA myself. I actually printed out the gazillion and two pages of the Act and curled up with it for a weekend. When I read it through the first time (yes, I said the first time; I've read it three times), I thought, oh my gosh, employers have no idea what's coming down the pipeline for them.

McDonald's hired me to do a feasibility study for a glimpse into how the ACA would affect their franchise owners, which ultimately led to my Ph.D. dissertation on compliance complexities that employers face under the ACA.

NavigateHCR began as a side hustle while I was still working full-time and in school. That time period was a lot like high school and college for me. I'd work from 6:00 a.m. to 2:00 p.m., have lunch and then work from three in the afternoon until midnight. And then do it again the next day. I was determined to get that damned doctorate! I finished in 2015 with a DBA and an 803-page dissertation.

Politics aside, the ACA and its implications for employers led me to the understanding that my job was to help American employers comply with its complexities.

I saw the handwriting on the wall (or the legislation, if you will). I took all of my consulting money, cashed out my 401K, downgraded my car, sold off purses and shoes online, and worked on the weekends to get NavigateHCR going.

It started taking off. We got way more business in one year than most people get in the life of their companies. For me, it was all about giving employers a solution to a highly complicated problem that—if they were not compliant—could put them out of business and in the poorhouse.

NavigateHCR began as a service company, but about a year in, I realized that to be scalable and help the most employers, it needed to be a software company. We transitioned a year later, and I'll tell you I could write a book called *How Not to Start a Software Company for Dummies* because I did everything wrong I could possibly do wrong.

In truth, I started the company to help other people get a chance—to get a YES instead of a NO.

I recently sold NavigateHCR, and it is now a part of U.S. Employee Benefits Services Group (USEBSG), a division of U.S. Retirement & Benefits Partners (USRBP). NavigateHCR will focus on developing new products and offering compliance measures to its clients.

It's my last company. I'm taking YES into the world. My answer today to practically anything is YES because everybody always gave me NO. I'm not going to stand in anybody else's way to do their job, live their life, grow their career, or find their passion.

I'm always going to say YES, and that's what this book is about. Saying YES to NO. No matter what.

Before we drop into the Nine NOtivational Nuggets, I want to point out that at the end of each chapter, I've included questions for you to ponder and answer about each topic, and room for you to take notes as you answer. This book will give you value if you read it, but this book will give you KICK ASS value if you do the work.

Let's get started. Your Million $ NOtivation is waiting.

ABOUT NOTIVATION AND YOU:

1. Connect with your past. Look at your relationships, successes, failures. In what situations did someone say NO to you? What did that create for you?

_____

_____

_____

_____

_____

_____

_____

_____

_____

_____

2. How does it feel when someone says NO to you? What is the result of NO for you?

_____

_____

_____

_____
_____
_____
_____
_____
_____
_____
_____
_____

3. What are the NOs that keep you clinging to limiting beliefs about what you can and can't accomplish?

_____
_____
_____
_____
_____
_____
_____
_____
_____
_____
_____
_____

4. What opportunities exist for you to change your NOs to YESes in the context of your life and business?

THE MILLION $ NOTIVATION

The mantra "Don't debate. Incorporate" is in many ways, my overarching business principle. The Nine NOtivational Nuggets support it. But the principle itself is always true for me, and I shout it from the rooftops to the women I mentor and support.

I'm OVER the inequality conversation. I'm OVER the equal pay discussion. I'm OVER being told NO.

DON'T DEBATE. INCORPORATE.

What does the principle mean? Exactly what it says. Stop arguing, stop listening to others who tell you what they think you should know or do, and just do your own thing already. Don't fall prey to the notion that women in business have to play small because (insert whatever bullshit reason here).

Women are still being told NO in the business world. But that doesn't mean you have to spend a ton of energy and time discussing it. Instead, get out there and live your biggest dreams, create your magic, NOtivate yourself, and make a ton of money. The NOs will turn to YES in the process.

I've written this book because that's not happening often enough right now. And we won't collectively change NO to YES until women-owned business revenue starts to compete with the boys.

Now, I know it's not easy to get any business to a million dollars in revenue. But for women-owned businesses, it's even more difficult.

THE EXTERNAL NO

The 2018 State of Women-Owned Businesses report from American Express takes a look at trends affecting and impacting women in business. While the number of women-owned businesses is increasing and stands at around 40 percent, total revenue from those firms is a sad, lackluster 4.3 percent.

In 2018, 88-fucking-percent of women-owned businesses generated less than $100,000! On the other tiny end of the spectrum, only 1.7 percent of women-owned businesses generated revenues of more than $1 million and employed a whopping 68 percent of total employment for women-owned businesses. The report calls those million-dollar-plus firms "economic powerhouses that made an outsized contribution to the economy."

That's a big-ass gap to fill.

Every woman who starts a business runs into gender-based obstacles. It's the nature of a system that was built by men, for men. I'm in the 1.7 percent and I still run up against those obstacles, as do my female revenue peers. We—the economic powerhouses—are in the process of changing it, but NO is still there waiting to discourage us.

I'll just list a few of the external, system-based NOs that impact women in business:

- Limited funding (many lenders still prefer men)
- Dual career-family pressures (she works as hard, but shoulders more of the responsibility and most of the guilt)
- Lower pay (often because women tend not to negotiate)
- Inadequate support availability (especially from mentors)
- Gender inequality (culturally, economically and politically, our business system was built by the boys for the boys)
- Gender bias
- Under-representation in key industries (think tech, finance, science)
- Inadequate promotion opportunities
- Lack of CEO level jobs

I could go on for pages, but you get the point, right? When it comes to making ourselves comfortable at the million-dollar business table, we women often have to bring our own chairs.

THE INTERNAL NO

It doesn't help our cause that we sabotage ourselves, sister. There's evidence that women score higher than men in key leadership traits. We hold more degrees, we multitask WAY better than men, we prioritize collaboration, we excel at creating relationships, and we're great at time-management. Yet in business, we are often our own worst enemies.

I'm heavily involved with Entrepreneurs' Organization (EO), which is a global, peer-to-peer network of more than 13,000 business owners in 185 chapters and 58 countries (as of January 2019). EO members must have annual revenue of at least $1 million. As you can imagine, our membership is not women-heavy either. In my San Diego chapter of 178 people, I'm one of only 14 women.

In mentoring other women striving for the $1 million ceiling, I'm sometimes shocked—but not really surprised—by the ways we tell ourselves NO before we even get a chance to drag our chairs to the table.

Seriously.

- We put everybody else's needs first
- We overthink and overanalyze

- We compare ourselves with men and each other
- We run from conflict
- We apologize unnecessarily
- We ask permission
- We undervalue our worth
- We undercharge
- We question ourselves
- We try to go it alone
- We don't negotiate or we under-negotiate
- We don't take risks
- We play small
- We lack confidence
- We fear being "salesy"

Do you see a pattern here? Right. So much of what keeps us from the table in the boardroom and the chair behind the CEO's desk is stuff we make up in our own heads, the fiction we write about why we shouldn't be there. We routinely and habitually tell ourselves (and each other) NO via our own deep, unintentional, often subconscious, limiting beliefs and behaviors.

I'VE GOT YOUR BACK

Here's something I learned early on in my career that illustrates the actual seat at the table and the ways women compare, compromise our own power, and sometimes are forced to adjust our behaviors to make others comfortable. I've never forgotten it, and I use it to this day.

This conversation happened when I was 26 or 27, with a woman older than me (I'll call her Mrs. Pruder, after my second-grade teacher), who I had just jump-frogged over position-wise. She said, "You are intimidating in meetings because you're so tall." (As I mentioned in the first chapter, I'm 6'2".)

I was kind of stunned and thought, well, how the hell do I change that? I mean, I was seriously asking myself the question, "How can I come across to people as LESS TALL?"

I feel that I'm extremely approachable, but my height does intimidate some people, so I've literally changed the way I stand next to others. If I'm with people—men and women—who are shorter than me, I usually take one or two steps back so that I'm not towering over them.

If I walk into a conference room and I'm the first person there, I will sit down. If a man shorter than I am comes in, I don't stand up and shake hands (which is appropriate for a woman but not for a man), so I don't come across as intimidating.

But if a man that I gauge is my height or taller enters the room, I stand up, shake hands and throw my tallness on the table—much like men metaphorically throw their penises on the table when they're jockeying for position. (More about that in NOtivational Nugget 7.)

FYI, I doubt that many men have asked themselves how they could make themselves LESS intimidating in the boardroom.

NOTIVATIONAL WISDOM

The NOtivational Nuggets on the following pages are the wisdom that works for me, and I hope some of them (or all of them) will help lay the foundation for you in your journey to your first million dollars.

But before we get there, I want to share one last lesson from the conversation with the proxy Mrs. Pruder, who told me I intimidated her. I think her conversation with me about my height was more about her than it was about me.

Instead of congratulating me on my promotion or saying, wow, you're really crushing it (like I would say to another woman), our conversation was about her discomfort with body language and her own limiting beliefs. She also complained about me sitting with my arms folded during meetings.

You know why my arms were folded? Because I was fucking cold!

Here's a bonus piece of wisdom. It's not one of my nuggets, and it should go without saying, but it doesn't, so I'm saying it; let's stop with those mean-girl stories we make up about ourselves and each other that sabotage our companies and employees and achievements. Let's replace them with one sentence that goes something like: "Girl, I got your back," and then quickly followed it with, "Don't debate. Incorporate!"

That's the Million $ NOtivation.

ABOUT YOUR MILLION $ NOTIVATION:

1. What are your external NOs?

_____

_____

_____

_____

_____

_____

_____

_____

_____

_____

2. What are your internal NOs? How are you sabotaging yourself?

3. What are you willing/unwilling to compromise on when it comes to your business and its growth?

4. Write down the annual revenue $$ amount for your company that rings your bells. What would you have to do to get there?

NOTIVATIONAL NUGGET 1

FUCK FEAR

I like to watch the TV show The Big Bang Theory. In an episode called *The Inspiration Deprivation*, female character Amy has been nominated for a Nobel prize, along with her husband, Sheldon. Amy is feeling the pressure of being a role model after someone reminds her that—because she is a girl—winning a Nobel prize could inspire a generation of female scientists.

Amy and Sheldon visit deprivation tanks to relax as they wait for the announcement. Sheldon blissfully floats in math nerd nirvana dreaming of numbers and huge sandwiches, while Amy lays there and imagines every possible way she could fail her fellow females.

We all know how she feels, right? Fear for women is sweaty palms and armpits and boobs and other inappropriate places. And we worry about shit that's not even ours, that we have no control over.

What's Amy's fear?

Failure. Letting other people down. No blissful dreams of celebration and sandwiches for Amy.

As I watched it, I thought, holy shit, that's exactly correct! What happens with women and fear is we start internalizing all the scenarios of our own lives and how we're failing our kids, our spouses, our parents, ourselves, the world.

Our fear creates self-sabotage, which is one way we tell ourselves NO before somebody else can do it.

MY FEAR ACRONYM

You've likely heard some commonly-used acronyms for FEAR. False Evidence Appearing Real. Face Everything and Rise. Forget Everything and Run.

Those don't resonate with me, so I created my own acronym for how I deal with fear. It goes like this:

Fuck It.
Embrace It.
Approach It.
Run to It.

FUCK IT

I've already shared with you that fuck is my favorite F-word. It's perfect. It's a noun, an adjective, a verb, and sometimes the only word that works.

In this case, I use the F-word to get me out of the paralyzing mindset that fear can create. Saying it out loud makes me laugh and, for some reason, negates the seriousness of whatever's happening that's causing me to feel fear. Once I laugh, I can say, all right, let's go, let's figure IT out— whatever IT is—the next company, or the next job, or the next hire, or whatever.

Fuck It calms me down and gets me balanced, so I can embrace whatever thought or experience is causing my fear.

EMBRACE IT

Embrace It really means wrapping my arms around the situation that's creating fear. It helps me figure out precisely what I'm facing.

For example, when I decided to sell my business, NavigateHCR, there was some fear involved. I knew the sale was inevitable, and I knew it was the right move, so I drew a line in the sand and stood firm.

I didn't second-guess my decision, I didn't overthink, I didn't get stuck in analysis paralysis. Instead, I moved toward the fear and the situation.

APPROACH IT

When I approach something that causes me fear, I'm really kicking the tires of the situation. When I was younger, I would try and analyze whatever was going on, which often created a powerless loop in my head. Stuck in the loop, eventually I would talk myself out of whatever it was, basically saying NO to myself.

However, when I Approach It rather than analyze it, I can go at it from a tactical standpoint and weigh the pros and cons and pluses and minuses. And because I'm not stuck, I can then Run To It.

RUN TO IT

Running to It enables me to do things I think most people would be held back from. I can't honestly say there's been a time in my life where I walked away from fear. I think I run towards it because I know that I can succeed, while I also know that failure is an option and that it's okay. It won't kill me.

In fact, fear excites me because it challenges me to say, "Oh yeah, I can do that." For all of the many situations where fear has come across my desk, or lodged in my head, or literally slapped me, I've looked for solutions.

So I Run to It and see what happens. And the result is inevitably one of two things: I succeed, or I fail.

I'm really good at both, so I fear neither.

FEAR IS A CHOICE

For me, fear and fearlessness are an attitude and a choice. I don't ponder the feeling of being afraid very often. When I do feel it, I use my FEAR acronym and make a move. It can take five minutes, ten minutes, an hour, or a day. I'm not a person who prolongs the conversation in my head or with other people for months or years.

Whether you're a seasoned business owner, working on your start-up, or just contemplating your next business venture, it's time to be fearless. It's time to get your fear out of your head, tell the Itty-Bitty-Shitty Committee that lives in your brain to cease and desist, stop talking about the things you can't do, and really start diving into what you want to do with your business.

ALLOW FEAR TO TEACH YOU

Fear can be a fabulous teacher. I learned this lesson well the first time I was served with a lawsuit. By the way, I always say that when you get sued, you know you've arrived.

I've been sued three times. The first time I was in my thirties and leaving one company for a new opportunity. The firm I was leaving was trying to get me on a non-compete. Here in California, you can't do a non-compete, and you can't stop someone's livelihood. But it's still a tactic that companies often use with salespeople jumping ship—it's a big fat NO.

That first lawsuit was kind of scary, as well as my first experience of hiring an attorney and navigating the process. It can be a long, drawn-out experience that sucks up time and money, especially if you choose to come at it from a fear-based perspective.

Sometimes you fight, and sometimes you compromise. I said Fuck It, Embraced It, Approached It, and Ran to It by finding a way not to go to court. It was a compromising solution that was not fair to anyone, but if I had stayed and fought the battle, it would have cost me more in effort, time, and money than I was willing to spend.

 I chose to compromise, take my lessons with me, and move on. What I learned in that first experience was to control the situation and put it on my timeline.

The next time someone sued me, I eliminated the feeling of drowning in paperwork and being held hostage to someone else's agenda by telling my attorney he could have access to me only on Fridays from 9:00 a.m. to noon.

YOUR FEAR IS COSTING YOU MONEY

Perhaps the highest cost of fear in the business world of women is the issue of equal pay. Why do I say that?

I've hired hundreds of women. I would say 90 percent of them DID NOT negotiate their salaries. There's NOgotiation happening, and I think the equal pay gap would be closer if women simply negotiated and valued their worth.

I ask everyone I hire—male or female—to give me their salary range. A man will give me an exact range. For example, $50K-$70K. A woman, on the other hand, will say something like, "Well, I was making $52K at my last job."

If I'm in the ballpark of a range, I typically offer in the middle of it. But if I know you made $52K at your last job, I'm probably going to offer $55K vs. starting in the middle of the range, which would be $60K.

I've negotiated every single commission dollar I've ever made. I've negotiated for more money, for PTO, for more vacation. And in my experience of hiring, 90 percent of women left something of value on the table because they simply didn't ask for it.

Is that fear? Is it a self-worth conversation? Is it a lack of confidence? Only they know.

But I know this for sure: it costs all of us.

PRACTICE FEARLESS REFLECTION

I heard something once that talked about the concept of fear and choice. It illustrated fear as a thing that exists only in our thoughts of the future, that fear is a product of our imagination and that while our fear FEELS real, there is no REAL danger from a thought. We just think we're in danger. Fear is a choice, brought about by stories we make up in our heads.

What story are you telling yourself when you feel fear? Is it a true story? Does actual danger exist?

Fear stops people from starting a business, and it prevents them from growing. I also believe most people, especially women, who get past the fear and start the business anyway do so from a fear-based perspective. And they take it right into the business with them with fear in the lead.

Knowing your core values, honing in on what you really want to create, whether you're starting or growing, is an excellent first step to allowing your fear to lead you rather than overwhelm you. Honestly reflect on your unique WHY and what's holding you back. Is it financial, fear of failure, imposter syndrome, lack of confidence, analysis paralysis?

For example, when I started NavigateHCR, I didn't tell myself and everyone else that I was creating a compliance software company because it's sexy. I went into compliance software because I wanted to protect American businesses. That's my core value, and it's a huge WHY. Holding steading to it held my fear at bay.

ABOUT YOU AND FEAR:

1. What's the FEAR acronym that works for you? Write your own or edit one of those I've listed.

_____

_____

_____

_____

_____

_____

_____

_____

_____

_____

_____

_____

2. What's your unique WHY, and what the fuck are you afraid of? Is it real or a story you're making up? Be honest.

_____

_____

_____

_____

3. Failure is a learning opportunity. What have you learned from failure, and what have you done differently because you failed?

4. Some people use a trigger word to calm yourself when you feel fear? If you don't have one, create one now.

_____

_____

_____

_____

_____

_____

_____

_____

_____

_____

NOTIVATIONAL NUGGET 2

SHIFT YOUR MINDSET

Don't announce to anyone that you're starting your own business until you metaphorically put on your Wonder Woman magic bracelets. You're going to need them to deflect and shield you as you grow your business and your own power.

As soon as you start your first business—or your next business, as I've learned—everyone's going to have an opinion about it. It will sound something like this:

"Oh, honey, why would you do that? We already have ten cupcake places in town."

Or, "My gosh, but you already have a great job. You're never going to earn that kind of money out on your own."

Or, "Nobody's going to want to do business with you. You don't know anything about that kind of thing."

You get the idea, and if you're a woman in business, I've no doubt you've had this kind of condescending, hurtful conversation with someone.

It's the world's way of telling you NO.

SHIFT THE CONVERSATION

I recommend that you stop to listen. But not to those people, the naysayers. Listen to yourself.

I've already told you about all of the times people said no to me in my life, who told me I couldn't succeed at algebra or college or whatever. It's been no different in business. People have scoffed at tons of my ideas, and my family probably thought I was crazy when I left the family business.

But I had this strong internal conversation that I've had since I was four years old, and I just didn't listen, and maybe more importantly, I never agreed with them. I don't even let that possibility play in my mind at all.

A lot of women listen to their spouses and friends, and that bitchy group of mean girls that lives in our heads that I call the Itty Bitty Shitty Committee. Remember Amy's Nobel Prize conversation from the last chapter? That's who she was listening to—that committee. Most

NO conversations are generated by stereotype driven expectations. Don't fall for it.

People mean well, really, and they think they're doing you a favor by sharing their opinion, but who has time or space for all of that negativity? Not me, sister. So I stopped talking to those people.

DEVELOP AN OWNER'S MINDSET

I didn't know this early in my career, and it's my hope that you'll get it now, wherever you are in your business growth and expansion: you must find people who are on a similar trajectory as you.

Let me repeat that. You MUST find people who are on a similar trajectory as you. The only people I talk to about my business now are my peers who own their own businesses and run in my revenue circle. They're mostly members of the Entrepreneurs' Organization (EO) that I mentioned in the last chapter.

We're a true business peer group. Not networking, not sales. We understand that we're each operating alone, on our particular island, if you will. She's got her island, he's got his island, and I have my island. When we come together, we all know exactly what it's like to be our own island. We talk about all of the business issues that we run into.

It's been game-changing for me to have a group of people that I know have been through the same things I have, who have succeeded and failed and maybe succeeded and failed again. And I know that they ultimately have the same mindset that I do, and it mitigates all of the other negativity that comes my way.

EMPLOYEE OR OWNER?

You may not agree with me, but I think a lot of people go into business on their own simply because they were shitty employees. I was a shitty employee. Are you? Were you? I mean, think about the business owners you know. Some of them are in business simply because they don't want anyone else to tell them what to do.

I also think many women start businesses because they're looking for flexibility, which is great and works for lots of us.

However, if you see yourself in either of those examples, I invite you to examine how you're thinking. Are you thinking like an owner or an employee?

When I had my first company, I was a young owner. Looking back on it, I did a ton of stuff wrong. I worked as hard, if not harder, than I did as an employee. Before I got into it, I think I thought it was going to be easier to be the owner than it actually was.

As the owner, you're buying the printer, you're changing the toner, you're finding and bringing in the clients, you're creating your book of business. There isn't anything in your company that you are not touching in some way.

In my twenties, I held on to stuff I didn't need to hold onto because I feared I wasn't competent or confident in what I was doing. I was still thinking like an employee. I guess I was young and dumb and paddling so hard to make money and survive that I was totally blindsided by the reality of the significance of what I was creating as a business owner. I realized, especially with a small company, the buck really does stop with me.

Once I hired my first employee, it was no longer just about me. In my thirties, I started to understand what it means to delegate and elevate. And that was where I came into understanding the people that work for me. I understood that they wanted to work with me on my team, and they wanted somebody to lead them. They have a mindset that if they're going to be working 40 hours somewhere, they want it to be for a reason and a cause.

When you're thinking like an owner, you realize and understand that you—your business, what you do—is affecting somebody's life positively or negatively. In a small business particularly, you get sort of tied to your employees' lives and families and everything that affects them.

From a big picture, you're also affecting the economy of the United States and the bottom line of the businesses you serve.

I had a Holy Shit moment the first time I understood the magnitude of what I had in my hands, the lives and families and livelihoods and careers and expectations and goals of others. For me, that's when my mindset shifted from employee to owner.

ABOUT YOU AND MINDSET:

1. When it comes to your business, whose opinions are you listening to and reacting to?

2. Who and where are the trusted advisers on the same trajectory as you? How will you connect with them?

_____

_____

_____

_____

_____

_____

_____

_____

_____

_____

3. What's your business mindset? Owner or employee? If it's an employee mindset, how will you shift it?

_____

_____

_____

_____

_____

4. How can you become a Teflon wonder woman in today's business environment and still stay true to you?

NOTIVATIONAL NUGGET 3

STAND TALL AND HARD TO YOUR CONVICTIONS

I know, I know, it's easy for me to tell you to stand tall because I am, but I really mean it. Put your shoulders back and straighten your spine, because as we've already established, in life and in business you're going to get rejected, to be told NO.

When I say Stand Tall and Hard to Your Convictions, I define conviction as the thing that stands tall in the face of uncertainty. It lives in your gut. It's the thing that made me shake my finger in the principal's face and say, "I am going to this school, and I'm going to college, and you're going to let me in."

Conviction is more than confidence. Standing tall and hard to your convictions means that no matter what, even if you don't know how it—whatever your 'it' is—is going to happen, you're going to follow it through to the end.

Standing tall and hard to your convictions reframes rejection, reframes NO.

BE GUMBY, DAMMIT

My mom bought me a Gumby doll when I was a kid. For those of you too young to know what a Gumby doll is, he is a bendable, posable, happy green character made of clay who had his own TV show way back in the day. And he's timeless; you can still buy Gumby online.

Gumby is totally resilient. My mom used to tell me, "You're Gumby, dammit!" (By the way, my Mom—the thief—stole and paraphrased the catchphrase "I'm Gumby, dammit!" from an 80s Saturday Night Live skit).

What she meant was that I bent and flexed with whatever came my way.

So yes, even though it might seem counterintuitive, I am telling you to stand tall and hard to your convictions while being flexible.

It's also about embracing what you can't control, defining your own path, and not allowing anyone else to pull you from it.

I don't know how I knew it in eighth grade, but I knew that high school and college were my trajectories. I couldn't control it; it wasn't my decision, but I showed up and fought for it.

I'm convinced conviction is the reason I passed algebra in my freshman year in college, as well. By being upfront with Dr. Stein about my limitations and being willing to do whatever it took, even though I'd learned by repeated failure that it was out of my hands, I passed and excelled in college.

LISTEN TO YOUR GUT. AND COLOR CODE IT.

Conviction lives in your gut. My gut has never steered me wrong. Have I made bad decisions? Certainly. I've also made plenty of excellent choices.

Even though I'm listening to my gut, I'm systematic about the approach. By that, I mean that when I'm working on an idea or a project or a process, I create plans and checklists. Once I get it on paper and flowchart it or color code it and can actually see it and visualize it, I always feel better about what my gut has to say.

BE REALISTIC

Many of us, as business owners, especially in the early days, will say, "I'm going to start a company, and I'm going to do 18 things in a day." (Do you recognize yourself here?) Yeah. It's just not realistic, and it starts you in a negative balance on your to-do list the next day. Conviction can get lost in that kind of chaos.

I am big on checklists and goals, and I also know I'm not here to change the world in one day. Women like you and I are in business to do big things. How do you do big things? You've likely heard the saying, "How do you eat an elephant? One bite at a time."

The only person I know who can successfully do 18 things in a day is my brother Jason, and he's been that way since the transplant. I don't even try to keep up with him.

I whittle down my goals, projects, and ideas to accomplish three things a day that move me forward. Conviction is all about how I keep moving forward.

CREATE YOUR OWN PATH

I've found that standing tall and hard to your convictions can mean stepping off the path of what's "normal and accepted" behavior and going your own way.

We'll all run into some kind of closed doors in our industries—they show up randomly in boardrooms and meetings and on golf courses and restaurants—and it's up to you to figure out how to open them.

For example, in my case, in my male-dominated industry, I decided long ago that I was never going to go golfing with the guys. It's not what I want to do, and I know they don't want to golf with me. What I've chosen to do instead is show up after the golf game is over, and have a drink or a meal with them. That's when the business gets done anyway.

Sometimes standing tall means that relationships end, as well. When I decided to move NavigateHCR from a consulting platform to software, I had a partner who didn't think that was the right move to make. I was convicted and trusted my gut. She was not on board with my vision, so I bought her out.

Even way back when I left my dad's company, I did so because of my convictions about the way people should be treated in business, whether that person is your daughter or your employee.

Conviction is the reason I started all of my businesses. I urge you to take a powerful stand for yours.

ABOUT YOU AND CONVICTIONS:

1. What are your convictions?

_____

_____

_____

_____

_____

_____

_____

_____

_____

_____

_____

2. Here's a formula to measure your convictions:
Convictions + Passion = $olutions. What's your passion,
and how will it lead to your solutions?

_____

_____

_____

_____

_____

_____

_____

_____

_____

_____

_____

_____

_____

3. What color resonates with you? How can you color-code and visualize the conviction that lives in your gut?

_____

_____

_____

_____

_____

_____

_____

_____

_____

_____

_____

4. If you were to create a toy character who represents you, what traits would that character have, and how would it serve you?

NOTIVATIONAL NUGGET 4

WHEN YOU FEEL YOUR WORST, LOOK YOUR BEST

"When You Feel Your Worst, Look Your Best," is a quote from my mom, Laura Kahle (I thought it was about time I told you her name since I'm revealing so many of her secrets).

My mom always said that to me during the many times I was down about not being able to grasp a subject or pass a test, or when I had to walk out to that fucking learning van with everybody looking at me. And she was right.

You might as well look good. Mom had this whole philosophy around it. I don't know how it works, but it works. On those days I don't want to get out of bed and show up for the world, instead of staying in my jammies I put on my best outfit, get my makeup perfect, and do my hair. It changes my whole thought process. I look good, and I start to feel good.

Hearing my mom say, "when you feel your worst, look your best," in my head never fails to pull me out of my pity party. And I don't think either mom or I knew it at the time, but back in the day, it also started preparing me to be a CEO.

DRESS LIKE YOU MEAN IT

For me, my mom's mantra fed my positive thought process. It was really about moving forward when all the chips were down. I'm a CEO that doesn't show my weaknesses or bad days or who gets bogged down in my failures, even though I've had plenty. I want my employees to know that everything's great, so let's keep throwing shit against the wall and see what sticks. For example, so we lost a large client, let's get three smaller ones.

I'm not talking about faking it (more about that in NOtivational Nugget 9). I'm talking about staying positive even on the days I don't feel like it. The alternative, in my mind, is to be negative. And who can talk shit to themselves in a great outfit and super cute boots? Not me.

Thank God my industry has lightened up, though. My first job was at a very strict insurance company where women were NOt allowed to wear pants and REQUIRED that women always wore pantyhose or tights with skirts and dresses. Can you imagine? No sandals or flats, only heels. And we had to have a jacket or blazer at the ready if clients came in.

That's not dressing like you mean it. It's dressing like somebody else means it.

Seriously, I owned NO JEANS whatsoever in the 90s.

Today, I showed up to an audience of 90 percent men looking like I know my shit, so my uniform is still pretty formal, but I choose it. And because it's basically my job to educate the masses about what will happen if employers aren't compliant, and show them how to pay $7 million rather than $22 million in fines, they take it better when the news comes from a smiling face in a flowered dress.

I dress for fun, but I support a very conservative industry.

THE DOUBLE STANDARD

You may have noticed the double standard that exists between men and women when it comes to looking good. I think the standard for men has deteriorated. Gone are the days of full-on suits, great ties, and dress shoes on men. Yet women are still held to a higher expectation of beauty and presentation.

I'm pretty particular about my female employees and how they dress, because again, we serve a conservative industry and because any business environment we enter is less than ten percent women. There's a continuing conversation about what is and isn't appropriate. But I don't REQUIRE them to dress like me.

And by the way, just for the record because someone has to say it and it might as well be me: khakis on men should be against the law. Please.

SHOW UP EVEN WHEN YOU'RE NOT 100%

Of course, there are days when the inner conversation doesn't match the outer appearance, right? What do you do then? I'm always the tallest, loudest, blondest woman in the room. I've had to get comfortable in my own skin. I know who I am.

Like every woman, even when I'm looking fabulous, I have days when I just don't want to do the thing. But like most of us, I don't often have the luxury of giving in to not doing that thing. So I walk into the room and in front of the crowd and present and represent.

Even then, I might be beating myself up internally and listening to the Itty Bitty Shitty Committee. My mom's mantra helps me remember to shut those bitches down and get my angels out. So I'll tell myself, hey, you're okay, you'll be fine! You've got great shoes on, and your hair is fabulous! I hear my mom in my head.

NETWORK LIKE THE BOSS YOU ARE

We've all got to network, right? It's not always fun. And again, sometimes I just don't want to do it. It doesn't happen often, but when it does, it's usually when I've been traveling, and I'm tired and don't feel like socializing.

And business is business, right? I'm an athlete; I'm goal-oriented and scoreboard oriented, so I play a game with myself—a numbers game. I set small goals, such as: go up to the bar, get a drink and say "Hi" to three people. Or get three business cards. Three is a magic number for me. Once I talk to three people, I can easily talk to and network with three more.

OR JUST TAKE THE DAY

I admit there are days that a designer outfit and red lipstick don't get me out of my funk. For me, if I'm in my funk for more than two hours, I just say fuck it and take the day. Get a massage. Go to the spa. Because girl, I get to do something for myself. And so do you.

ABOUT YOU AND LOOKING YOUR BEST:

1. What's the one thing you don't leave the house without? Lipstick? Mascara? How do you feel without it? With it?

_____

_____

_____

_____

_____

_____

_____

_____

_____

2. What's your "looking good" mantra? Steal mine, or write your own.

_____

_____

_____

_____
_____
_____
_____
_____
_____
_____
_____
_____
_____
_____

3. How do you show up even when you're not 100%?

_____
_____
_____
_____
_____
_____
_____
_____
_____
_____

4. What's your favorite "just take the day" activity that's sure to get you out of your funk? And when was the last time you did it? (If you don't know, do it tomorrow.)

NOTIVATIONAL NUGGET 5

BE YOUR OWN HERO, DOROTHY

Recently, I had what's become a fairly common conversation in my life while at the airport in Louisville waiting on a flight. I sat next to a young woman who was furiously typing away on her computer. We chatted.

She told me she's working nine to five for a big online retail company based in Las Vegas, living there, flying back and forth to their outlet in Louisville, and trying to start a business at the same time. Obviously, she needs money to pay the bills. She's got a job, she's got a kid, she's got a husband. Sound like anybody you know?

We discussed all of the things that are derailing her from starting her business.

I shared my story and how when I started my first business, I would wake up every morning at 4 a.m. and work on my company stuff until 7 a.m. That was *my* time. And then I would work on other people's business or pay the bills from 7 a.m. to 7 p.m. and then do it again the next day.

I reminded her that if starting a business is her vision and that's where she's headed, she has to figure out how to get to that goal without letting life events and distractions derail her and put her in the fetal position. Or without creating situations where she's feeling victimized by circumstances, or giving her power away, or handing over control to someone else because she feels like she doesn't have any.

I would like to say to her and to you, as Glinda the Good Witch said in the *Wizard of Oz*, "You've always had the power to go back to Kansas, Dorothy."

You're the Good Witch of your own story. And the Good Witch is powerful.

CHOOSE POWER

Before we get deep into looking at power, I just want to point something out. Do you ever see men walking around with notebooks or wearing t-shirts or jewelry that says, "Boss Man," or "Empowered Men Empower Men," or "Nevertheless, He Persisted"? Fuck no, you don't see them.

But there's a whole slew of women out there who do, and it's basically to remind themselves that they're powerful. I think it's because we tend to give our power away, and need a reminder that truly, we hold all the cards, and that we can take back our power as many times as we give it away.

I'm a force to be reckoned with now, but I didn't magically become that way. I'm committed to supporting women in getting back their power by sharing my story, sharing my failures, sharing my defeats, and all of the other painful experiences that depleted my power.

I don't necessarily share my successes because I don't feel the wins really connect you to your strength. It's navigating the shit—the NOs—that makes you a woman of power.

WE ALL HAVE SHIT. WHAT'S YOURS?

I'm using the term shit here as sort of a synonym for trauma because I don't want to go down a psychological rabbit hole in talking about the devastating and myriad experiences that we women allow to derail us from our visions and dreams.

I'll use this definition: a traumatic event is an incident that causes physical, emotional, spiritual, or psychological harm. I'm bringing it up because we all have some version of trauma and injury that can disrupt us and pull us off our path. How do we continue on the way, yet deal with and be realistic about all the shit that goes on in our lives?

Unfortunately, quite often we keep our traumas and hurts hidden, thinking that's the way to defeat the emotion we think diminishes our power. Yet talking about it often increases our power.

My most defining shit moment happened when I was a junior in college, and I've only started sharing it in the last few years.

In a nutshell, my college boyfriend—he was older, and I was in love with him—kept me in a room for 24 hours and beat me. I got away, went straight to the police, and reported it. They took me back to campus in a cruiser. The next day, bruises and all, I played the best game of my basketball career.

At the time, I was 21 years old and didn't understand the magnitude of my own power. I knew, though, that I would never allow a man to do that to me again and that I would not allow him to do it to somebody else. I took my ex to court and sent him to jail.

For me, it's really become a lesson about giving my power away, taking it back, and then flexing that power, using it.

THE STRENGTH OF FORGIVENESS

After that incident, I realized I didn't want to be a victim. I didn't want to walk around angry, and once I had my power back, I felt the most authentic thing that I could do with it was to forgive my abuser.

He was in jail for six months and got out at the beginning of my senior year. He reached out to me then. He'd also sent me letters while he was in jail, but I'd thrown them away unopened.

I think he'd been out maybe two or three months when I decided I would meet him in a public place in Boston and actually talk to him and have a conversation. He wasn't looking for forgiveness, but I walked in prepared to give it without him asking for it.

We talked briefly. It wasn't eventful. I left but asked him to stay in the restaurant and not follow me. I told the bartender I was leaving, and asked him to be sure my ex stayed there for at least 10 more minutes. I walked out, jumped in a cab, and away I went back home to my college campus.

And then I tucked the experience away and didn't talk about it for more than twenty years.

I don't know why I didn't talk about it. Once I finally did share it, I was surprised at the depth of emotion that came with it, and the funny thing is, I wasn't anticipating sharing it. I just felt like it was the right time—the safe time. And I didn't anticipate the amount of heartfelt response I would get back about it, either.

As I've continued to share that story, I've been surprised to know it inspires other women or sometimes leads them into their own power or invites and gives them permission to be vulnerable and share their own story. I didn't expect that at all.

For me, when I SHARE my pain and mistakes, I stand in my power.

ABOUT YOU AND POWER, DOROTHY:

1. What's your shit?

2. What's the story that you're not telling because you think it makes you look weak or vulnerable?

3. Name one person you would like to forgive. Do it here on paper.

4. Describe how it feels to be powerful. Describe how it feels to be powerless. How does each of those show up in your business?

_____

_____

_____

_____

_____

_____

_____

_____

_____

_____

_____

NOTIVATIONAL NUGGET 6

GROW A FENIS

There are days you just have to throw your dick on the table. Metaphorically speaking. And in a feminine way, of course.

I'm sort of kidding. But really, because I'm a woman with 20 years of experience in a man-heavy industry, I've often been in situations (especially in sales meetings) that I felt at a loss as to how to flex my power. I mean, I don't have a penis to compare to the other penises in the room. I don't know if you've seen it, but that version of metaphorical male competition happens daily in board and conference rooms.

The urban dictionary defines "throwing your dick on the table" as: "Similar to putting your foot down, 'putting your dick on the table' is a phrase used when someone exerts their dominance over everyone else in the room."

I think the first time I realized I was going to need something more to throw on the table was early in my career. I realize lots of women may never run into this situation as heavily and repetitively as I have, but as a woman in business, you will, at some point, be in the position of deciding what you need to bring to the table in order to compete.

I see evidence of it all the time in my EO business group. I've already mentioned that members are required to have at least $1 million in revenue, and we have 178 members. Again, only fourteen are women.

Imagine a scenario where I introduce a male business owner to a female business owner in my EO group. In the first five seconds, the man is going to talk about his business, how much he makes, his car, his wife, his girlfriend, etc. He basically just puts it all on the table.

Most women in my group are the opposite. Clearly, they're making at least $1 million or they wouldn't be present, but even so women are either uncomfortable talking about their revenue or they don't know how to sell themselves and their business. We're all basically on the same economic playing field. But women react entirely differently than men. Sara Blakely, the founder of Spanx, is in our group, and when she first started, even she didn't enter with her own power.

For me growing a Fenis (which is your version of a female penis) is really about how you powerfully compete with men. If you want to have the same kind of conversations and be taken seriously, you have to learn to throw it down, to some extent, in a way that's comfortable for you.

For me, it's about how I can bring my energy to a meeting, or bring my particular power to a male-dominated conversation. Women really want a perspective from men, but it gets a little tiresome when it's all about one-upping and muscle-flexing.

DEFINE YOUR FENIS POWER

I have a highly developed sales Fenis. I had two realizations sitting around male-dominated sales boardrooms in my twenties. One: all salespeople lie, including me, in a sales situation. And two: men flex their strength to exaggerate and compete.

They'll say, "I'm closing this before you do. It's a done deal." They're optimistic and outsized (surprised?) about their possible results, where women are much more cautious. A man will say, "Yup, that sale is ninety percent closed," while a woman would call it fifty percent closed.

I quickly got tired of hearing men talk about what percentage they were going to close, and instead, I'd go to the meeting with the sale already closed. They were still trying to make the deals, and I was done. That was the way I learned to throw my sales muscle on the table.

I also like to throw down my brain. You might say my big head thinks better than my little one, instead of the other way around. Because even now that I'm doing fewer sales and more consulting, training, and teaching, the male muscle-flexing and penis throwing still show up quite a bit.

Every once in a while, when I'm teaching or talking with someone, there's that guy that walks in the room and wants to dominate the conversation because he thinks he knows more than I do. I don't remind him that I've read the ACA three times, I just let him take his penis (his self-perceived superiority) out and show it to the entire room.

It reminds me of playing college basketball. So many girls talked trash on the court. But I just let my game show. My talent then was shooting. I knew I was always going to score between fifteen and thirty points, and I let the scoreboard speak for me.

So how I handle that guy now is by bringing up a theory he doesn't know or a process we've perfected, letting him understand he doesn't know as much as he thinks, but not verbally. You might say I muscle him around a little.

You define your Fenis power with your strengths. I know I'm strong in sales, I work harder than anybody else works, and I know how to take a very complicated process or law and whittle it down so the masses can understand it.

I'm always going to bring results to the table. That's my Fenis.

ABOUT YOU AND YOUR FENIS:

1. What's your strength? And if it's not your dick (metaphorically), what are you throwing on the table? How are you going to play with the boys?

_____

_____

_____

_____

_____

_____

_____

_____

_____

_____

2. How do you react when someone else throws his or her Fenis on the table? Is it working for you? If not, how can you change it?

_____

_____

_____

_____

_____

_____

_____

_____

_____

_____

_____

3. Draw your Fenis. What does it look like?

NOTIVATIONAL NUGGET 7

PANTSUITS ARE FOR BUSINESSMEN AND MONKEYS

Did I just call men monkeys? Yup, and it's so appropriate after you've just drawn your version of a Fenis.

Because honestly, even though I've told you to grow a Fenis, that's the only add-on I'm going to recommend that's masculine (unless that's your look and intention, then, by all means, go for it).

There's a quote by Coco Chanel that goes, "Dress shabbily, and they remember the dress; dress impeccably, and they remember the woman."

Am I saying you should wear a dress? Or never wear a pantsuit? Nah, girl. Or maybe, if that's where your power lives. What I am saying is no matter what you wear, stop trying to fit in. Do You, Boo, because there's POWER in being you.

PANTSUITS DID NOT WORK FOR HILLARY

Before the pantsuit became a pantsuit, a suit was just a suit. A pantsuit, in my opinion, is a uniform for women that is acceptable to men.

And I think it's one of the ways Hillary (and I mean Hillary Clinton, in case you're from Pluto) lost credibility. I believe the visual impression she left on people was harsh because she was portraying herself as someone who "fits in" in the male world of politics. In doing so, she gave away her power.

Impeccably dressed women (and men) who define their style also define their power. Think of Michelle Obama. Kate Middleton. Kerry Washington. They clearly found their lane, defined it, and stayed there. You know them by their look and their consistency in creating it. Standing out, knowing who you are, and defining how you show up is a power play.

How are you using yours?

WHAT'S YOUR UNIFORM?

My uniform is pretty; it's soft and bright and fun. I wear jackets and sweaters and dresses, and I'm relatively conservative—again because I serve a traditional industry.

I can easily do a hundred dresses in a row without wearing the same one.

My uniform works for me. I stand out in my industry. I mean, anybody can wear pants, right?

It's interesting to me that when and if I shift from my power dress to pants my entire dynamic shifts. When (and if) I wear a pantsuit, I know I can hide; I can sit in the back and blend in with everybody else.

Are you blending in or standing out? I've had many women tell me they wear pants to work because they don't want guys staring at their legs. I'm here to tell you if they do that, it's their issue, not yours. I'm an athlete and a jock, but because I want to stand out in a man's world, I'm embracing my femininity in the workplace.

And it works. But there was this one time…

It pisses me off to even have to tell you this story, but I'll tell it anyway.

THE STRAW THAT BROKE THE CAMEL'S BACK

I'm the camel. Stereotypes and misogyny are the straw, in this case. And this version of being told NO really kicked me into starting NavigateHCR.

It was 2012—so NOT the dark ages—and I was working for a company I didn't have any ownership in (I was sold to it in a buyout), but of course, I was a Top 10 producer for them.

Before we were married, my future husband Hector and I were in Hawaii with the company at a dinner banquet for the top producers. In the insurance industry, most companies send their top salespeople to Hawaii to celebrate them. We were on Maui. (I now own a beach condo there; it's my happy place.)

Anyway, I was wearing this amazing Kate Spade pink and orange dress with fabulous heels, and I was smoking hot. We were at the awards dinner, at the table for the top producers, and people (men) started coming up to Hector, walking right past me, and congratulating Hector on being a top producer.

Hector played them, being funny and saying things like, "Yeah, insurance is tough." And, "Wow, employee benefits are really challenging."

The first time it happened I was like *well, that's weird*. And then it happened again, and again, and again, and by the fourth time, I was fucking STEAMING mad.

Now mind you, the men congratulating Hector on his achievements weren't just some company flunkies. They were LEADERSHIP, company executives who should have known that I—not Hector—was the top sales producer. Monkeys.

When it came time to be recognized, I was in the top five to be called, and I walked on stage to collect my award (the only woman, of course) and stayed for the usual group picture.

Normally in a picture environment, I scoot to the back because everyone is either my height or shorter than me, but not this time. I chose to stand front and center with my award.

I didn't know it until later, but that picture was never published. After we all got back from Hawaii, pictures of the trip went out via email to the entire company. Not one picture was from that awards ceremony. There were only two women in the top 50 producers, but the company employed plenty of other women. Don't you think they would have loved to see a picture of another woman on stage? They didn't see it.

The message was clear. I didn't fit in because I wasn't a man. I wasn't good enough to be seen.

NOT MY CIRCUS, NOT MY MONKEYS

I decided right then and there that I would never be sold again, and I would never put myself in an environment like that again.

Hector and I went back to our hotel that night, and I said, "I am not going to be with those people anymore." I canceled every event and activity I was scheduled to attend during the company trip.

I chalked it up to just another one of those things that happen in my industry, but I was done with that company. It took me about six months to leave. I'm mixing my animal metaphors, but that straw created by executive male monkeys eventually became NavigateHCR and the reason I make it my business to employ women.

In fact, if I was giving advice to a young woman who was starting a business in a male-dominated industry—and let's be realistic, all business is still male-dominated—I would tell her to find her power early and experiment with it and tweak it as she goes. Define it, own it, and stand in it. It's yours.

And oh, by the way, I changed the karma of that amazing dress and wore it to my rehearsal dinner. And I'll never forget those shoes.

Fuck blending in.

ABOUT YOU AND STANDING OUT:

1. What's your uniform? What does it say about you?

_____

_____

_____

_____

_____

_____

_____

_____

_____

2. Are you standing out or blending in? If you're standing out, how can you strengthen your power? If you're blending in, what's keeping you there?

_____

_____

_____

_____

_____
_____
_____
_____
_____
_____
_____
_____
_____
_____

3. Who are the women you emulate for their style and power? Why? How can you create your version of what you admire in others?

_____
_____
_____
_____
_____
_____
_____
_____
_____

4. Who are the monkeys in your business world, and how do you stand in your power among them

_____

_____

_____

_____

_____

_____

_____

_____

_____

_____

NOTIVATIONAL NUGGET 8

YELL YOUR STORY FROM THE MOUNTAINTOPS

When I say "Yell Your Story From the Mountaintops," I mean it.

From now on, when it comes to promoting yourself and your business, I want you to get good at it. We women are notoriously bad at telling our stories, at singing our own praises, at tooting our own horns.

Promoting yourself isn't hard. Remember that.

We—women—do not engage others in what we're creating in the world. Instead, we tell people what we do.

As you know, because I've said it a bunch of times, I protect American businesses. That's what I'm creating, what I'm putting into the world. What I DO is own a software technology company. Do you see the difference?

It's always fascinating to me when I ask a woman what she does. She'll say, "I sell clothing." Or "I do copyright law." Or "I do blah. Blah. Blah." What she's *not* saying is, "I'm a business owner."

We've talked about how men throw down their proprietorship (and perhaps their penis) on the table. The first thing they say is, "I own my own business." It's a key and interesting dynamic difference between men and women.

I was coaching a girlfriend about this. She says, "I'm in PR." And I say, "Yeah, but you own a PR company. So let's try this again. What do you do?" And she's like, "I'm in PR." And I say, "No, again. How about, 'I own a PR agency in San Diego.' Try something like that."

It took her four or five tries to even just talk about the fact that she's a business owner.

This, sister, is not serving us. It's just another way we tell ourselves NO.

IT'S LEARNED BEHAVIOR

Promoting your business in everyday speech is learned behavior. Not doing it is learned behavior as well. The trick is noticing and unlearning what's keeping you from yelling your story from the mountaintops.

Come on! You've worked hard! Talk about it!

Women in business excel at execution, but we're not so good at promoting ourselves. Recent research shows that seventy-six percent of women in leadership positions identified inadequate self-promotion as a major obstacle to professional success.

I get it. I didn't tell anybody about my first business. I think it was because I felt like maybe I didn't know what I was doing, so I didn't necessarily want to hear anybody confirm that.

There are lots of reasons women are uncomfortable talking about their accomplishments, and it's partly because women have historically been called aggressive for blowing their own horns. Not so for men.

I think it's about lack of confidence, an unwillingness to look dumb, feeling discounted, all the little things that add up to us shutting up. I also think we just don't really know how to have the conversation. I certainly was in that space when I started NavigateHCR.

TEST PILOT YOUR STORY

We've all heard we should carefully craft our elevator speech. I don't think you need to necessarily have an elevator pitch, but I think you need to know clearly what it is you say about your business so that others understand what you do and/or are curious enough to ask follow-up questions.

I came up with the tagline, "I protect American businesses," through trial and error, and seeing what stuck. Because NavigateHCR provided a completely fresh product that was created in response to legislation, and that nobody knew anything about, I tested it through conversation, and I did it with anybody and everybody—not necessarily only with those who would be buying my products.

I mean, if you're a soda company, there's not a lot to figure out, right? Everyone knows it's soda. But I needed to find a way to explain what we did and how we were going to do it and what it ultimately resulted in. I really wanted to some extent use people as test monkeys to get the verbiage down that best described our products and the business.

The number one question we ask each other in business and social situations is, "What do you do?" so I used every situation—dinner parties, networking, travel conversations— to float various ways to describe the business until I landed on what worked. I'd talk about the name of the company, what we do, what we ultimately ended up doing, and maybe one or two of our products, just see if people could understand what it was we were doing.

I also used people in my industry as test monkeys as well; interestingly, it was advice and ideas from those outside my industry that ultimately gave me the verbiage I'm using now.

I let them teach me how to craft a simple message that works for our buyer.

HORSESHOE COMMUNICATION

I'm sure you've noticed in networking that women tend to gravitate to other women. When you walk into a networking group, you often walk into a room with circles of people talking. Circles do not instill inclusion.

One of the things that I've really focused on is making sure that in any situation, the people I'm talking with feel part of the group. There are no circles in my world, only horseshoes, so others feel free to walk into any conversation.

It's one of the ways we can tell each other YES and support each other in yelling our story from the mountaintops.

ABOUT YOU AND YOUR STORY:

1. Why do you think women, in general, are so afraid to tell people they're business owners? Is this you?

_____

_____

_____

_____

_____

_____

_____

_____

_____

_____

2. What's your answer when someone asks you what you do?

_____

_____

_____

_____

3. How and with whom can you test pilot the story of your business? Not what you do, but what you create and provide to the world?

4. Where do opportunities exist for you to create horseshoe communication?

NOTIVATIONAL NUGGET 9

DON'T FAKE IT, JUST MAKE IT

You've heard that old saying, "Fake it till you make it," right? I fucking hate that saying.

Why? Because if you're trying to grow and improve your business, the last thing you should be doing is faking anything. And maybe it's because I've been around so many men that do fake it. And because I think we women sometimes give our own authenticity away with our power.

I'm going to use another TV show to illustrate my point (I know, I watch a lot of TV for someone who recently sold her company, NavigateHCR, for an EIGHT TIMES return!). In case you don't know this, the average return is one or two times! I made millions of dollars on that sale. Authentically. On my own. *I made that happen.*

FAKING IT

Anyway, the other day, I was watching a documentary-style reality TV show that featured a female business owner who was dating the sales guy (her employee).

She let him make decisions for her, and he led her down the wrong path. She was $2.4 million in debt, and her conversation about the company was all bullshit. She was saying everything was great, that she had tons of orders coming in, but in reality, she had lenders threatening her personally, a car that was repossessed, and an eviction notice on her door.

As I was watching, I was wondering, my gosh, how many other women business owners are out there faking it?

If you're faking it, you're genuinely not making it. NOt making it.

THE STRUGGLE IS REAL

The reality is that business owners struggle, and women in particular often don't have any idea about where to go for help, what to ask for, or how to ask for it.

We all get into ruts. Being willing to ask for help before your debt is $2.4 million and your car gets towed, and your sales boyfriend rips you off, is being vulnerable enough to say, "Help! I'm not making it."

I know this because there were plenty of times I didn't ask for help, didn't let anyone know I was struggling. What I learned was I had to be willing to NOT CARE what other people thought about me.

I think a lot of business owners keep up the pretense that everything is "fine." Everything's great, and everything looks good, and it has to be that way because they want everyone to believe they've got their shit together.

Guess what? Nobody has their shit together. Not one single person has their shit together all the time, including me.

If you're that "fine" business owner, I invite you to get real, get vulnerable, and start telling the truth about what's actually going on.

That looks like trusting your person—the one who's on the same trajectory as you (NOtivational Nugget 2)—with your reality. Like, here's what keeps me up at night. Or I'm struggling with sales, or I'm struggling with marketing. Or I hate my employees this week. Or I can't make payroll, and I'm paying myself zero.

Business owners find themselves in all sorts of struggles, but because we live in this social media, everything-is-perfect kind of environment, they don't share their struggles, so they never ask for help.

For me, when I've gotten vulnerable and real and shared my own battles, I've received way more back in blessings in the way of ideas, contacts, suggestions, and solutions than the little bit of pride or shame it cost me to ask.

DON'T FAKE IT, JUST MAKE IT

And when I say make IT, I mean make some MONEY. Refuse to be told NO. If that's your environment, go around it.

I made my first million when I was twenty-eight years old. It was pretty cool. I took thirteen-ish accounting courses in school, and I thought at one point, I was going to be an accountant. Thank God I'm not because I'd be bored, and wearing monkey suits and pantyhose.

I do remember what it was like watching that ticker counting up to my first million. I saw $800K, and then $900K, and then when I finally hit one million and maintained it, I was like, damn, that's a lot of zeros.

With my second company, it took me less than a year to reach my first million. I'd done it once, so I knew how to do it. And with my third company, NavigateHCR, we skyrocketed from zero to $1.4 million in like six months. It was crazy, crazy growth. And as I mentioned earlier in this chapter, I got an EIGHT TIMES return on it.

Now THAT'S a shit-ton of zeros!

You make it, sister, like I did. By taking risks. By throwing shit against the wall and seeing what sticks. By showing up, no matter how you feel. By saying "fuck you" to fear and "watch me" when somebody—anybody—tells you NO. By being vulnerable and asking for help. By whipping out your Fenis and bringing your own authenticity and power to the table.

THE POWER OF NO

We tend to think of NO as a negative. But you know, for me—the dyslexic—back in the day when I heard the word NO, I saw it as ON, and that meant keep going. Keep keeping ON.

I got so sick and tired of hearing NO at every turn that ON became my answer to it. (Maybe I should have called this book One Dyslexic Girl's Journey to ON, lol.)

And eventually NO and ON became YES. As I may have mentioned, nobody tells me NO these days. Even so, women are still collectively hearing NO from the business world.

Let's work together to change it by sharing our own stories. What's not being told out there are the stories of women like me who are making it every day, growing their businesses to six and seven and eight and fifteen million dollars.

We're sort of in this no man's land (pun intended) because we don't see news about the people that are doing it every day. We're not making waves, right? We're just doing our shit. We're just going out and doing our business and doing what we need to do.

Now more than ever, I'm seeing more women stepping up to help other women, and I don't feel like that has ever happened in these numbers.

And you know why? Because enough is enough. I think a bunch of us are just done. We're just done talking about it, and we're doing it.

That's my final advice to you. Get NOtivated to do your own fucking thing and say enough is enough to letting someone else control your net worth!

ON, sister.

ABOUT <u>YOU</u> AND MAKING IT

1. What does making it mean to you?

_____

_____

_____

_____

_____

_____

_____

_____

_____

_____

2. How are you faking it? How are you not telling yourself the truth?

_____

_____

_____

_____

_____
_____
_____
_____
_____
_____
_____
_____

3. What NOtivates you?

_____
_____
_____
_____
_____
_____
_____
_____
_____
_____

4. What opportunities exist for you to support other women business owners, and if you're not already doing so, when will you begin?

EPILOGUE

A little story about negotiation:

My brother Jason may soon need a kidney. I am, of course, a perfect match. But I'm no longer a feisty four year old without negotiation skills.

As my price for a kidney, I've designed a stunning set of jewelry (I got nothing for that bone marrow, remember?).

In a perfect world, Jason will wake up healthy and craving my drinks of choice—wine and maybe a bit of fireball whiskey—and I'll be the only sister in the world with custom-designed rose gold kidney-shaped earrings and a necklace.

ABOUT THE AUTHOR

Dr. Kristin L. Kahle (aka Dr. K) is the CEO and Founder of NavigateHCR (NHCR), a full-service human resources and compliance technology company. She is a speaker and author who is doggedly passionate about helping others in business, especially women.

Dr. K started her first company while still in her 20s and has since started and sold two more companies; all three businesses sold for well over seven figures.

Dr. K laments a decided lack of female mentors and coaches during her career. Partly because she was so much on her own, she'll tell you she did everything wrong in learning to get it right, hence her passion to help others.

Dr. K is the first Doctoral candidate to write on ACA/Employer Compliance Complexities. In 2014 and 2015, she was awarded the "Most Influential Woman in Benefits" by Employee Benefit Advisor. More recently, she was nominated for the San Diego Business Journal Top Tech Award 2019. Passionate about her employer clients, Dr. K also started a non-profit, HEEL, Help for Employers and Employees Under ACA Legislation, through which she serves as a lobbyist on Capitol Hill.

Dr. K holds a DBA from Argosy University, an MBA from the University of Phoenix, and a BA from Pine Manor College. She is well-known for being the only female athlete at PMC to obtain a double-double (scoring and rebounding) in basketball.

Linkedin.com/in/drkristinkahle

Facebook.com/drkkahle

www.ingramcontent.com/pod-product-compliance
Lightning Source LLC
Chambersburg PA
CBHW030526210326
41597CB00013B/1048